Can I tell you about Parkinson's Disease?

Can I tell you about...?

The "Can I tell you about...?" series offers simple introductions to a range of limiting conditions. Friendly characters invite readers to learn about their experiences of living with a particular condition and how they would like to be helped and supported. These books serve as excellent starting points for family and classroom discussions.

other subjects covered in the "Can I tell you about...?" series

ADHD

Asperger Syndrome

Asthma

Dementia

Dyslexia

Epilepsy

OCD

Selective Mutism

Stuttering/Stammering

Can I tell you about Parkinson's Disease?

A guide for family, friends and carers

ALAN M. HULTQUIST

Illustrated by Lydia T. Corrow

Jessica Kingsley *Publishers*
London and Philadelphia

First published in 2013
by Jessica Kingsley Publishers
116 Pentonville Road
London N1 9JB, UK
and
400 Market Street, Suite 400
Philadelphia, PA 19106, USA

www.jkp.com

Library of Congress Cataloging in Publication Data
Hultquist, Alan M.
Can I tell you about Parkinson's disease? : a guide for
family, friends, and carers / Alan M. Hultquist ;
illustrated by Lydia T. Corrow.
pages cm
Audience: 7+
ISBN 978-1-84905-948-0 (alk. paper)
1. Parkinson's disease--Juvenile literature. 2. Parkinson's
disease. I. Corrow, Lydia T., illustrator. II.
Title.
RC382.H85 2013
616.8'33--dc23
2013010975

British Library Cataloguing in Publication Data
A CIP catalogue record for this book is
available from the British Library

ISBN 978 1 84905 948 0
eISBN 978 0 85700 767 4

Printed and bound in Great Britain

This book is dedicated to Brendan

Acknowledgements

I offer thanks to my former colleagues Liz Audette, the wonderful J. and Nancy Roberts James. They read an early draft of a different, but related, manuscript and provided the encouragement that kept me working. I also need to thank my longtime friend Robin Stander for her help in getting the final draft ready.

A special thank you goes to Diane L. Church, PhD, at the Dartmouth-Hitchcock Medical Center (DHMC). I emailed the New Hampshire American Parkinson Disease Association Information and Referral Center at DHMC asking if anyone there might be willing to check over an early draft. Dr Church responded immediately and got back to me within a few hours with suggestions, comments and answers to questions. Thank you for responding to a complete stranger's request that someone read his manuscript. I do not know if you realise just how rare and valuable your response to that situation was.

My husband, Brendan Hadash, has been at my side all through this process. You had no idea what you were getting into when we first met in 1983. In addition to your love and support, your help with this book was invaluable.

Finally, although people offered comments and suggestions about the manuscript, the responsibility for the final content, including any errors and omissions, is entirely mine.

This book is not intended as a source of medical advice. There are many conditions that can look like Parkinson's disease. Any diagnosis and treatment must be done by a qualified and licensed professional.

Contents

"I usually call it Parkinson's, or just PD for short. I'd like to tell you what it's like, what it feels like and how you might help me."

"When we first meet, you might not notice there are things about me that are different from other adults. But after a few minutes, you'll probably start to see that I move and act a bit differently from what you expect. Like everyone else, people with PD are individuals, and PD affects each person differently. So, other adults with Parkinson's will be like me in some ways, but not in others.

Having Parkinson's means I don't do some things as well as I used to. My main problems are with remembering, being organised, sleeping and getting my body to do what I want it to do. But I can still do other things without difficulty. How easily I'm able to do something sometimes depends on whether or not my medication is working."

"Parkinson's disease is a medical problem that affects my brain, but I wasn't born with it. No one is."

"Everyone's body is made of cells, which are very, very tiny. I have PD because some of my brain cells died. Those cells used to make one of the chemicals my brain needs to communicate with my body. Without enough of that chemical, it's now harder for my brain to work properly and tell my body what to do.

I started having trouble when I was in my 40s, and a doctor told me I had PD when I was 50 years old. She looked for four signs or symptoms to find out if I had PD. These were shaking, slow movement, stiff muscles and difficulty with balance. But PD can also cause many other problems.

Parkinson's gets worse over the years, but I'll be telling you about some of the things I can do to help me stay active for a long time.

It's important for you to know that you can't catch PD the way you catch a cold or flu. You can shake my hand and drink from the same glass as I do, but you won't get Parkinson's."

"Some parts of my body shake a lot."

"Shaking is one of the most common signs of Parkinson's disease, but not everyone with PD shakes.

I first knew I needed to see a doctor because my right hand began to shake when I wasn't actively using it. In the beginning, my hand only shook occasionally, but over the years it began to shake more often. The medicine that I now take helps. If I don't take it, my right hand will shake all the time while I'm awake. However, even when I take my pills, my hand still shakes if I'm nervous, worried, angry, really happy or excited. My legs, left hand and head have started to shake sometimes too.

Actively using my hand stops the shaking. So, it might shake when I'm walking or holding a book, but not when I'm painting or using a keyboard. If my hand is shaking for any reason, I can make it stop by fidgeting with something, like a coin or a small ball. However, as soon as I stop actively using my hand, the shaking starts again."

"I have stiff muscles and often move slowly."

"My muscles don't move easily. Therefore, I don't walk as fast as I used to and I don't take big steps. I also don't always pick up my feet. Instead, I sometimes slide and drag them. Walking isn't something most people have to think about. But if I want to walk correctly, I have to think to myself, 'Nikolai, pick up your feet and be careful where you step.' I also don't swing my arms when I walk unless I think, 'Nikolai, remember to swing your arms.'

Even though I have trouble walking, I can still ride a bicycle. Doctors think steady, regular patterns, like cycling, make it easier for someone with PD to move. That might be why I walk better when I listen to the rhythm of a metronome or to music with a good beat.

Many of my other muscles are also stiff and hard to move. I blink less often than most people do. My handwriting can be small and hard to read. And my face might look the same whether I'm happy, sad or angry.

I help my muscles stay flexible by doing stretching and other exercises every day."

"Sometimes, I have trouble
keeping my balance."

"Most people don't have to worry about falling down. Their brains know how to keep their bodies steady no matter what they're doing. I used to be the same, but now I can fall easily.

I might lose my balance when I turn around, stand up, bend over, put on a coat or just about any time I move. I might also fall if someone bumps into me. My brain simply has a hard time telling my body how to keep steady all the time.

I can also lose my balance when I'm walking. If this happens, I lean forward and start taking short, quick steps. It might look as if I'm trying to run. I usually end up falling.

Because my balance is no longer very good, I don't use stepstools or ladders any more, and I always hold onto the railing when I use stairs. I try to think about my posture and remind myself to stand up straight. I also use a cane or walking stick sometimes to help prevent falls, especially if the ground is uneven or slippery."

"Sometimes it feels like my feet
are glued to the floor."

"I can be walking along and then, without any warning, my feet won't move. This can happen when there's a change in my walking route. I might need to turn a corner, go through a doorway or walk into a narrow space. Maybe the floor changes from wood to carpet, or perhaps there's something in my way. I can see the change coming, but my brain can't tell my body how to adjust to it, so my feet just stop. The doctors call this 'freezing'.

Once in a while, if I wait for a few seconds, my feet will 'unfreeze'. But I usually have to trick them into moving. I might pretend there's something on the floor to step over, or shift my weight from side to side before I step forward. I could say '1-2-3-go' and then start walking, or hum a song and move to the music. I might create a movie in my mind of someone marching, and then get my body to match that movie. Or perhaps I'll move some other part of my body before trying to move my feet."

"I have a hard time pulling words out of my memory. I also have trouble doing more than one thing at a time."

"Sometimes I have trouble thinking of the words I want to say. I haven't forgotten them, but they've become lost in my mind and I have to search for them. When that happens, I might stop talking in the middle of a sentence. Also, when someone asks me a question I might not answer right away because I have to get my thoughts together.

I have a hard time keeping track of what I'm doing if I try to do too much at once. For example, if I put laundry in the washing machine and then go shopping, a few days might go by before I remember to take the clothes out of the machine.

I work around my memory problems by trying to focus on doing only one thing at a time. I also keep a small notebook in my pocket so I can write down things I need to remember. And I have a wristwatch that vibrates to remind me when to take my medicine."

"I'm not as organised as I used to be, and it's hard for me to handle interruptions."

"If I have more than a few things to do, I can have trouble planning how to do them. It's best if I keep a consistent schedule, but that isn't always possible. At work, I meet with my boss every morning to plan my day. She also checks with me now and then to see if everything's going okay. My family helps the same way at home.

If I'm working on a task and someone interrupts me to ask a question or needs me to help them with something, I can have a hard time getting back on track. After the interruption, my thinking might freeze and I can have trouble deciding what to do. When this happens I need a mental push to get back to what I was doing. Sometimes, I can give myself the push, but other times I need someone's help to get back to work. And I might have to go back to the beginning of my project and start over."

"I have a lot of trouble sleeping at night."

"I often have trouble falling asleep because of something called 'restless legs'. I get unpleasant feelings in my legs that only go away if I move them. Unfortunately, the feelings come back as soon as I stop. It's hard to fall asleep when I have to keep my legs moving all the time.

Sometimes I wake up because of painful cramps in my feet. I also have very real dreams. When these happen, I move around in bed as if I'm acting out the dreams in my sleep. I don't wake up, but this kind of sleep isn't restful.

The medicines I take for Parkinson's also make it hard for me to sleep well. They aren't meant to do this, but it happens anyway. When medicines do something unexpected, it's called a 'side effect'.

I help myself sleep better by getting plenty of exercise during the day, relaxing in a warm bath before bed, meditating, listening to restful sounds and by going to bed and getting up at the same times every day. There are also medicines that help me sleep."

"The pills I take for Parkinson's
don't work perfectly, so how well I
move changes during the day."

"Because PD gets worse over the years, I now have 'on' times and 'off' times. 'On' times happen when the medicines are working well. When I'm 'on', it might look as if I don't have any physical problems. When I'm 'off', I suddenly begin to shake, my face loses some expression, and my walking gets slow. 'Off' times happen when the medicines are wearing off or aren't working as well as they should. Because I take PD pills every three hours, there are many times each day when I move between being 'on' and being 'off'.

Having too much medicine get into my brain too quickly can also cause problems. When this happens, parts of my body start to twist, bend and move in other ways I can't control. This stops after my brain uses up some of the medication.

My doctor and I work together to make sure I'm taking the right amount of medicine at the right times of day. We meet regularly to talk about how I'm doing and to make changes in my medication."

"Taking medicine isn't the only way I help my PD symptoms."

"One of the most important things I do every day is exercise. I use a treadmill and resistance bands to keep fit. I stretch and do yoga to help prevent my muscles from getting too stiff. I also do T'ai Chi to work on balance, strength, coordination and movement.

I spend time every day exercising my brain. I play card games. I do number puzzles and crosswords. I also enjoy solving logic problems.

I don't let PD stop me from doing the things I want to do. I walk to the store, go out to eat and go to the movies. I also like to travel and visit new places.

I look for the positive things in life and for ways to laugh about PD. For example, if I fall when I'm walking across a lawn, I might make a joke about tripping over a blade of grass. Also, if I can no longer do something the way I used to, I find a different way to get it done. I don't let PD get me down."

"Many people ask me what it feels like to have Parkinson's disease."

"When the doctor told me I had PD, I felt surprised because no one else in my family has it. I also felt worried because she said there wasn't a cure and the PD would get worse over time. Sometimes, I was angry because my future wasn't going to be what I'd hoped for. I still feel frustrated occasionally when I can't do things as well as I want to.

Often people ask if PD hurts. The answer is both 'yes' and 'no'. At first, I didn't have any pain, but now my stiff muscles can hurt. Sometimes I have painful muscle cramps in my feet. My eyes are often dry and sore because I don't blink very often any more. The restless legs that keep me awake at night are also a kind of pain. So sometimes Parkinson's hurts and sometimes it doesn't.

I go to a support group for people with Parkinson's and we talk about how things are going. Being able to talk with other people who have PD has helped me look at Parkinson's positively and to feel good about myself."

Ways people can help

"Let me tell you some of the ways you can help a person who has Parkinson's disease."

WAYS EVERYONE CAN HELP

- "Ask the person with PD if they want help before you do something for them.

- Don't try to hurry them. Be patient and understanding when they're slow, frozen or forgetful.

- When someone with PD freezes, don't force them to move. You could encourage them to use some of the tricks I mentioned earlier. You could also lightly tap the top of their shoe, or use a laser pointer to make a spot of light on the floor right in front of their feet so they have something safe to try to step over. If the person with PD often freezes in the same places at home, such as when approaching doorways, you could put a series of horizontal lines of tape on the floor. The colour of the lines should contrast sharply with the colour of the floor so they're easy to see. You should get help from a therapist to make sure you get the lines placed properly.

- When someone with PD is talking with you, look at them and turn off your music, TV or video game so they can concentrate better.

- Learn the Heimlich manoeuvre, because some people with Parkinson's have trouble swallowing and can choke on food.

- If they tend to fall a lot, hold onto their arm when they walk or stand up.

- Wait until they finish what they're doing before you interrupt them.

- Help the person with Parkinson's remain active. Ask them to go for a walk, go swimming or invite them to play a sport with you. Also, invite them to do fun things, like play games, go to a movie, go out to eat or visit a museum.

- Help the person who has PD with gardening or household chores.

- Ask them what they would like to do, and then do it with them.

- Treat the person with Parkinson's the same way you treat everyone else."

MORE WAYS FAMILY MEMBERS CAN HELP

- "Encourage the person with Parkinson's disease to be as independent as possible.

- Make the home safer by reducing clutter and getting rid of rugs and other things the person with PD might trip over. Create straight-line walking paths and install grab bars, floor-to-ceiling safety poles and other aids when necessary.

- Don't nag the person with Parkinson's. For example, don't keep telling them to stand up straight, pick up their feet or talk more loudly.

- Attend a support group for people with PD and their families. These are great places to get advice, learn about treatments, share stories, laugh, ask questions and make new friends. You might also want to talk with a professional counsellor.

- Talk openly with each other about problems that come up.

- If the person with PD has a poor memory, you could remind them to write things down, make a 'to do' list for them, give them only one thing to do at a time and try to make sure they have a consistent schedule.

- Be their exercise partner every day. Don't just remind them to exercise, but do the exercises with them."

ADDITIONAL WAYS CARE PARTNERS CAN HELP

- "Go to medical appointments with the person who has Parkinson's so you can ask questions and take notes.

- Accompany them when they see their physical or occupational therapist to learn about ways you can help.

- Make time for yourself every day. You need to be rested and feeling good if you are to help the person with PD. You could use tools such as the *Caregiving Distress Scale* and the *Caregivers Stress Inventory: Self Assessment* (http://parkinson.org/Caregivers/PD-Caregiving-101.aspx) to help examine how you feel, what levels of support you have and what additional support you need.

- Be sure there is someone you can call for help.

- Be willing to accept help when friends and family offer it."

More information about Parkinson's disease

"There are many things you might want to know about Parkinson's disease.

- PD gets its name from James Parkinson. He was a physician in England about 200 years ago. He didn't have PD, but he wrote an article that described some people with the physical symptoms of the disease.

- About three out of every one thousand people have Parkinson's. About seven to ten million people worldwide have Parkinson's.

- PD usually starts after the age of 50, but according to *The Encyclopedia of Parkinson's Disease* (Mosley, Romaine and Samii 2010), about 5 to 10 per cent of people with PD develop it earlier than that.

- *Young-onset* Parkinson's begins between the ages of 20 and 40. However, some people extend that age range up to 50.

- *Juvenile-onset* PD begins before someone is 20 years old, but that's very rare.

- Some people with Parkinson's inherit it from one of their parents, but most people with PD don't have a close family member with the disease.

- Parkinson's develops very differently from one person to the next. Doctors can't predict how fast the disease will progress or which of the many problems that comes with PD a person will have.

- The physical symptoms of PD first show up on one side of the body. After a few years, they also appear on the other side, but usually not as bad.

- Daily exercise is important for everyone with PD. It helps their brain work better and can help slow the speed at which the physical symptoms progress.

- Some countries have laws requiring that employers make adjustments so people with disabilities, such as someone with Parkinson's, can keep working."

THE FIRST SIGNS OF PARKINSON'S

"Doctors can't diagnose PD until the physical symptoms appear. However, most people with Parkinson's have other difficulties well before then.

- Early symptoms of PD include trouble with memory, organisation, concentration, word finding and sleep.

- For many people, an early sign of PD is losing the sense of smell.

- Not everyone who has these problems will develop Parkinson's.

- According to *The Encyclopedia of Parkinson's Disease* (Mosley, *et al.* 2010), these symptoms can have 'on' and 'off' periods just like the physical symptoms do."

STIFF MUSCLES CAN CAUSE LOTS OF PROBLEMS

"Living with Parkinson's can be challenging because the stiff muscles make doing many things difficult, such as the four mentioned earlier: walking, blinking, writing and showing facial expressions. However, the stiffness can also affect every muscle in the body.

- This stiffness can:

  ○ make it hard for someone with PD to button clothes, tie shoelaces, get out of bed, eat, comb their hair, brush their teeth and do other things that let them be independent

  ○ cause problems with eye movement, and that can make reading and driving difficult

  ○ make it hard for someone to speak loudly and clearly

  ○ make swallowing difficult.

- Stiff muscles inside the body can make food move through the stomach and intestines very slowly. This can make it hard for someone with PD to eat enough. It can also cause constipation.

- Stiff muscles inside a person's chest can make it hard for them to breathe correctly.

- Because it's hard for people with Parkinson's to move, and because they often have to think about what they want their body to do, they can get tired easily."

PARKINSON'S DISEASE CAN AFFECT THE ENTIRE BODY

"The longer someone has Parkinson's, the more parts of the body it can affect. PD can:

- make a person shake on the inside as well as making their hands, legs or head shake

- cause someone to sweat too much or too little

- make someone often feel as if they need to urinate

- make it hard for a person to have a consistent body temperature, so they might be too hot sometimes and too cold at other times

- cause skin rashes or make someone's skin either very dry or very oily

- cause vision problems. Some people with PD have blurred or double vision. Some have trouble seeing in dim light. Others might not be able to see an object if it's almost the same colour as its background. For example, they might not see a white dinner plate on a white tablecloth. And some people with Parkinson's see things that aren't really there

- cause people to think and react slowly. They can also have trouble making decisions

- cause people to develop a lack of interest in doing things, even fun things. They can also have problems with depression and anxiety

- cause some people to have trouble controlling their emotions, so they might laugh or cry at the wrong times."

SOME WAYS DOCTORS CAN HELP

"There isn't a cure for Parkinson's disease yet and it doesn't go away, but there are ways doctors can help.

- At first, a doctor usually gives a person with PD pills to take a few times each day. These pills stop the physical symptoms. However, because Parkinson's gets worse as the years go by, the person needs to take more pills and needs to take them more often. Depending on how old the person was when they developed PD, eventually the doctor has to try other treatments.

- One of these other treatments is a sticky patch that the person puts on their body. It's about the size of a large adhesive bandage or sticking plaster. The patch contains medicine, and the person's body absorbs that medicine through their skin. People who use this patch have to change it every day.

- Another treatment involves having a small tube put into the person's belly. The tube connects to a small pump strapped to their waist. The tube and pump keep a steady flow of medicine going into the person's intestines. People who use this treatment don't wear the pump when they sleep.

- Sometimes doctors do brain surgery to help someone with PD. The doctor puts a tiny electrical device into the person's brain. The doctor then connects that device to a small battery and computer chip in the person's chest by running a very thin wire under their skin. This device sends an electrical pulse to the person's brain to help stop the shaking and to let them move more easily. Some people have two devices and batteries, one for each side of their body. A doctor needs to replace the battery every few years.

- Many people are working hard to come up with new treatments, so other approaches could be coming soon."

OTHER SUPPORTS FOR PEOPLE WITH PD

"Doctors aren't the only ones helping people with Parkinson's disease.

- Physical therapists (or PTs) help people with Parkinson's move better. A PT can also work with them to develop an exercise programme that targets specific skills or that works on general fitness, such as improving strength, endurance and flexibility.

- Occupational therapists (or OTs) help people with PD remain independent. An OT can help them find new ways to complete daily tasks (such as bathing and dressing), and go to the person's home to help them figure out what changes to make so they can keep living there and to make the home safer. An OT can also make suggestions for people at their place of work.

- Speech therapists help people with Parkinson's when they have trouble talking, breathing, swallowing or using nonverbal communication, such as facial expressions.

- Experts in complementary approaches who are also knowledgeable about Parkinson's disease can help some people gain symptom relief. Complementary approaches are used in addition to more traditional ones and can include specific types of massage therapy and yoga, mindfulness and other forms of meditation or relaxation, and T'ai Chi Ch'uan, along with music, dance and art therapy. The person with PD should talk with their neurologist before beginning any kind of complementary treatment.

- Assistance dogs (or service dogs) can be a big help for some people with Parkinson's. These dogs get special training. They can help 'unfreeze' someone's foot by tapping it with their paw. Assistance dogs wear a harness with a handle for the person with PD to hold onto. This helps them keep their balance. The dogs can also tell when the person is losing their balance. When that happens, the dogs act to help keep the person upright. If the person does fall, these large, strong dogs know where to stand so the person with PD can use them as a support as they stand up. Assistance dogs can also help with daily activities, such as picking things up, turning on lights and opening doors. They can even learn when and how to push an emergency call button. And because dogs need to go for a walk every day, they help the person with PD get exercise."

Some words to know

If you read other books about Parkinson's disease, talk with a doctor or speak with someone who has PD, you might want to know some important words. If a definition contains a word in *italics*, you will also find that word in this list.

Agonist (AG-uh-nist): a kind of medicine used for PD. There are many different agonists. The brain treats them as if they were *dopamine.*

Amantadine (uh-MAN-tuh-deen): a medicine that was first used for flu, but is now also used for PD. Doctors think it helps the brain make more *dopamine.*

Basal ganglia (BAY-zul GAIN-glee-uh): the part of the brain where the *substantia nigra* is located.

Bradykinesia (BRAY-dee-kuh-NEE-zuh): slow movement.

Bradyphrenia (BRAY-dee-FREE-nee-uh): slow thinking.

Carbidopa (CAR-buh-DOE-puh): a medicine that helps *levodopa* work better.

Chronic (KRON-ik): something that lasts a long time. PD is a chronic disease.

Cognitive (COG-nuh-tiv): having to do with thinking. Difficulties with memory and organisation are part of the cognitive *impairments* that come with PD.

Cogwheel resistance (ree-ZIS-tins): one of the two kinds of stiff muscles that come with PD. Unlike *lead pipe resistance,* cogwheel stiffness isn't smooth. It's jerky and irregular. When someone tries to move the arm or leg of a person with PD who has cogwheel resistance, the way their muscles move feels rather like a car driving over a road with a lot of small bumps placed close together.

COMT inhibitors (in-HIB-uh-ters): a type of medication that helps *levodopa* work longer.

Deep brain stimulation (STIM-you-LAY-shun): a treatment for PD where doctors put a small electrode in the person's brain and connect it to a battery in their chest.

Degenerative (dee-JEN-er-uh-tiv): getting worse over time. PD is a degenerative disease.

Dopamine (DOE-puh-meen): a chemical (or *neurotransmitter*) that the brain needs to work properly. The *substantia nigra* makes a lot of dopamine. By the time someone finds out they have PD, up to 80% of the *neurons* in the *substantia nigra* have died. The brain uses dopamine to help the body move smoothly. Other *neurotransmitters* are also involved in PD.

Dyskinesia (dis-kuh-NEE-zuh): unwanted body movements (such as twisting and swaying) that happen when there's too much *levodopa* getting into a person's brain.

Dysphagia (dis-FAY-juh): difficulty swallowing.

Dystonia (dis-TOE-nee-uh): painful muscle spasms and cramps.

Fatigue (fuh-TEEG): feeling as if your arms and legs have weights attached to them, or feeling a large lack of energy.

Festination (FES-tin-AY-shun): leaning forward and suddenly walking with short, increasingly rapid steps that usually lead to falling.

Freezing: not being able to move when you want to.

Gait (gate): the way a person walks.

Hallucination (huh-LOO-suh-NAY-shun): seeing, hearing, tasting, feeling or smelling things that aren't really there.

Hypophonia (HI-puh-FOE-nee-uh): a speaking voice that's soft and weak.

Idiopathic (ID-ee-oh-PATH-ik): a disease that happens for no known reason. Most of the time, PD is idiopathic because most people don't inherit it from their parents.

Impair, impairment (im-PAIR; im-PAIR-mint): made weaker or worse. PD impairs a person's ability to walk, move and think.

Impulsive behaviours (im-PUL-siv bee-HAIV-yurs): behaviours that happen without the person stopping to think about them first. A side effect of some PD medications is the development of impulsive behaviours such as, gambling, excessive shopping, overeating and so on.

Insomnia (in-SOM-nee-uh): lots of trouble sleeping.

Lead pipe resistance (ree-ZIS-tins): one of the two kinds of stiff muscles that come with PD. Lead pipe stiffness feels like a continuous, smooth struggle when someone tries to move an arm or leg of a person with PD. It's different from *cogwheel resistance*.

Levodopa (LEE-vuh-DOE-puh): a medicine used for PD. The body uses levodopa to make *dopamine*.

Masked face: showing little or no facial expression.

Micrographia (MY-crow-GRAF-ee-uh): small, cramped handwriting.

Motor: having to do with moving. Walking, running, writing and drawing are examples of motor skills.

Movement disorders specialist (MOOV-mint dis-OR-ders SPESH-uh-list): a *neurologist* who works with people who have trouble moving properly, such as people with PD.

Neurologist (noo-RALL-uh-jist): a doctor who helps people when their brains aren't working properly.

Neurological (noo-ruh-LAW-jik-ul): having to do with the brain, nerves and nervous system. Parkinson's is a neurological disease.

Neurons (NOOR-ons): a kind of cell found in the brain and nervous system. One kind of neuron makes *dopamine*.

Neurotransmitters (NOO-row-TRANS-mit-ers): chemicals that the brain uses to make sure all parts of the body are working properly. *Dopamine* is a neurotransmitter.

Orthostatic hypotension (OR-thoe-STA-tic HIE-poe-TEN-shun): a sharp drop in blood pressure when a person stands up. It can cause dizziness, lightheadedness or fainting.

Pill-rolling: a kind of *tremor* where the thumb and fingers rub together as if the person were rolling a pill between them.

Postural instability (POS-ter-ul IN-stuh-BIL-uh-tee): trouble with balance.

Progressive (pruh-GRES-iv): to keep moving along in a series of steps or stages. Parkinson's is a progressive disease. There are various ways to look at how PD is progressing. Some *neurologists* use the "Unified Parkinson's Disease Rating Scale". Some people with PD find the "Parkinson's Well-Being Map" helpful (www.parkinsons-voices.eu/well-being-map).

Pseudobulbar affect (SUE-doe-BUL-bar AF-fekt): sudden, uncontrolled laughing or crying that might not match how the person really feels or that might be too intense for the situation.

Rigidity (ruh-JID-uh-tee): stiff muscles.

Substantia nigra (sub-STAN-shee-uh NIGH-gruh): a part of the brain that produces *dopamine*. It's located in the *basal ganglia*.

Tremor (TREM-er): shaking.

Wearing-off: the period between doses of PD medication when symptoms return because the current dose is wearing off and the next one has not started to work yet.

Some helpful books

Here are some ways to find out more about the brain and Parkinson's disease.

BOOKS FOR YOUNGER CHILDREN

Curry, D.L. (2003) *How Does Your Brain Work?* New York: Children's Press.

Jenkins, K.M. (2008) *Who Is Pee Dee: Explaining Parkinson's Disease to a Child.* Atlanta, GA: UCB.

In this book, a panda bear explains Parkinson's disease to a young child and mentions some ways he can help his mother, who has PD.

Lennard, K. (2006) *Young Genius: Brains.* Hauppauge, NY: Barron's Educational Series.

Rodriguez, C. (2012) *The World According to Honey Bear: A Doggone Good Read.* La Jolla, CA: PublishingGurus

This book explains Parkinson's disease from the point of view of an assistance dog.

Silverman, B. (2007) *Who's in Control: Brain and Nervous System.* Chicago, IL: Raintree.

BOOKS FOR OLDER CHILDREN AND TEENS

Abramovitz, M. (2005) *Parkinson's Disease (Diseases and Disorders).* Farmington Hills, MI: Lucent Books.

Parker, S. (2009) *Brain (Body Focus: Injury, Illness, and Health),* 2nd edn. Chicago, IL: Heinemann.

Silverman, B. (2007) *Who's in Control: Brain and Nervous System.* Chicago, IL: Raintree.

Vander Hook, S. (2001) *Parkinson's Disease (Understanding Illness).* North Mankato, MN: Smart Apple Media.

BOOKS FOR ADULTS

Ahlskog, J.E. (2005) *The Parkinson's Disease Treatment Book: Partnering with Your Doctor to Get the Most from Your Medications.* New York: Oxford University Press.

Brackey, J. (2007) *Creating Moments of Joy: A Journal for Caregivers,* 4th edn. West Lafayette, IN: Purdue University Press.

Friedman, J.H. (2013) *Making the Connection between Brain and Behavior: Coping with Parkinson's Disease,* 2nd edn. New York: Demos Medical Publishing.

Mosley, A.D., Romaine, D.S. and Samii, A. (2010) *The Encyclopedia of Parkinson's Disease,* 2nd edn. New York: Facts on File.

Parashos, S., Wichmann, R.L. and Melby, T. (2012) *Navigating Life with Parkinson Disease.* New York: Oxford University Press.

Peterman Schwarz, S. (2006) *Parkinson's Disease: 300 Tips for Making Life Easier.* New York: Demos Medical Publishing.

Weiner, W.J., Shulman, L.M. and Lang, A.E. (2007) *Parkinson's Disease: A Complete Guide for Patients and Families,* 2nd edn. Baltimore, MD: Johns Hopkins University Press.

Some exercise resources

People with Parkinson's disease need to exercise regularly. Their family and friends should encourage them and exercise with them. Everyone should talk with their doctors before doing any type of exercise. If someone with PD is unable to go to an exercise class or gym, they might find the following DVDs helpful, as long as their physician approves. They might also need to talk with a physical therapist before starting an exercise programme.

AM/PM Yoga for Beginners (www.bodywisdomdvds.com).

Beginning Tai Chi with Patrick Martin (http://esp.extended.nau.edu/TaiChi.aspx).

Motivating Moves for People with Parkinson's (www.parkinsonheartland.org/mmoves.html).

Move It! An Exercise and Movement Guide for Parkinson's Disease (http://parkinsonsmoveit.com).

Parkinson's Disease & the Art of Moving (www.parkinsonsexercise.com)

Parkinson's UK *Keeping Moving – Exercise and Parkinson's* (www.parkinsons.org.uk/advice/publications/day-to-day_living/keeping_moving_-_exercise.aspx).

People who don't have a DVD player or who want to bring an exercise programme with them when they're away from home might find the following resources helpful.

Chronicle Books: This company (www.chroniclebooks.com) sells some decks of exercise cards, such as *The Stretch Deck* and *The Yoga Deck*.

FitDeck: This company (www.fitdeck.com) sells a variety of decks of exercise cards, including *FitDeck Stretch*, *FitDeck Senior*, *FitDeck Resistance Tube* and *FitDeck Travel*. They also have a booster pack called *FitDeck Office* for people who want suggestions of ways they can exercise at work.

Parkinson's UK *Keeping Moving – Exercise and Parkinson's* Booklet (www.parkinsons.org.uk/advice/publications/day-to-day_living/keeping_moving_-_exercise.aspx).

Move It! An Exercise and Movement Guide for Parkinson's Disease: The author (http://parkinsonsmoveit.com) sells an exercise book in addition to the DVD listed above.

Parkinson's Disease & the Art of Moving: The author (www.parkinsonsexercise.com) sells an exercise book in addition to the DVD listed above.

Parkinson Home Exercise: This is an app for the iPhone, iPod Touch and iPad. It includes videos of various exercises and movement instructions designed to help with specific issues, including walking, posture, standing up, balance, bed mobility, flexibility, physical condition and relaxation. It includes a metronome.

Recommended organisations and websites

The following information was correct at the time I wrote this book.

ASSISTANCE/SERVICE DOGS

Assistance Dogs International
PO Box 5174
Santa Rosa, CA 95402
USA
www.assistancedogsinternational.org
Email: info@assistancedogsinternational.org

COMPLEMENTARY AND ALTERNATIVE TREATMENTS (US)

National Center for Complementary and Alternative Medicine
9000 Rockville Pike
Bethesda, MD 20892
USA
www.nccam.nih.gov
Email: online form
Phone: +1 888 644 6226

WORKPLACE ACCOMMODATIONS (US)

Job Accommodations Network
www.askjan.org
Email: online form
Phone: +1 800 526 7234

RESEARCH UPDATES

Also see the list of Parkinson's disease organisations.

Michael J. Fox Foundation for Parkinson's Research
Grand Central Station
PO Box 4777
New York, NY 10163–4777
USA
www.michaeljfox.org
Email: online form
Phone: +1 800 708 7644

Parkinson Research Foundation
5969 Cattleridge Blvd, Suite 100
Sarasota, FL 34232
USA
www.parkinsonresearchfoundation.org
Email: info@parkinsonresearchfoundation.org
Phone: +1 941 870 4438

Science Daily
www.sciencedaily.com/news/mind_brain/parkinson's/headlines

PARKINSON'S DISEASE ORGANISATIONS FOR INFORMATION, REFERRALS AND SUPPORT

UK

Parkinson's UK
215 Vauxhall Bridge Road
London
SW1V 1EJ
UK
www.parkinsons.org.uk
Email: hello@parkinsons.org.uk
Phone: +44 (0)808 800 0303

Republic of Ireland

Parkinson's Association of Ireland

Carmichael House
North Brunswick Street
Dublin 7
Ireland
www.parkinsons.ie
Email: info@parkinsons.ie
Phone: +3531 800 359 359

USA

American Parkinson Disease Association

135 Parkinson Avenue
Staten Island, NY 10305
USA
www.apdaparkinson.org
Email: apda@apdaparkinson.org
Phone: +1 800 457 6676

American Parkinson Disease Association, National Young Onset Center

Central DuPage Hospital
25 N. Winfield Road
Winfield, IL 60190
USA
www.youngparkinsons.org
Email: apda@youngparkinsons.org
Phone: +1 877 223 3801

APDA Rehab Resource Center at Boston University

College of Health and Rehabilitation Sciences: Sargent College
635 Commonwealth Avenue, 6th Floor
Boston, MA 02215
USA
www.bu.edu/neurorehab/resource-center
Email: online form
Phone: +1 617 353 7525

Movers & Shakers Inc.
880 Grand Rapids Blvd
Naples, FL 34120
USA
www.pdoutreach.org
Email: online form
Phone: +1 239 919 8287

Muhammad Ali Parkinson Center & Movement Disorders
St Joseph's Hospital and Medical Center
240 West Thomas Road, Suite 301
Phoenix, AZ 85013
USA
www.maprc.com
Email: online form
Phone: +1 800 227 7691

National Parkinson Foundation
1501 NW 9th Avenue/Bob Hope Road
Miami, FL 33136–1494
USA
www.parkinson.org
Email: contact@Parkinson.org
Phone: +1 800 473 4636

Parkinson's Disease Foundation
1359 Broadway, Suite 1509
New York, NY 10018
USA
www.pdf.org
Email: online form
Phone: +1 800 457 6676

Parkinson's Resource Organization
74–090 El Paseo Suite 104
Palm Desert, CA 92260
USA
http://parkinsonsresource.org
Phone: +1 877 775 4111

Canada

Parkinson Society Canada
4211 Yonge Street, Suite 316
Toronto, ON M2P 2A9
Canada
www.parkinson.ca
Email: general.info@parkinson.ca
Phone: +1 800 565 3000

Australia

Parkinson's Australia
PO Box 717
Mawson
ACT 2607
Australia
www.parkinsons.org.au
Email: CEO@parkinsonsaustralia.org.au
Phone: +61 0407 703 328

New Zealand

Parkinson's New Zealand
PO Box 11 067
Manners Street
Wellington 6142
www.parkinsons.org.nz
Email: info@parkinsons.org.nz
Phone: +64 0800 473 4636

Other

In addition to supplying information about Parkinson's disease, these websites combined offer names, contact information and/or links to PD information and support organisations in over 30 countries around the world.

European Parkinson's Disease Association
1 Northumberland Avenue
Trafalgar Square
London
WC2N 5BW
UK
www.epda.eu.com/en
Email: info@epda.eu.com
Phone: +44 (0)207 872 5510

Parkinson's Voices
www.parkinsons-voices.eu/home

World Parkinson Disease Association
via Zuretti 35
20135, Milano
Italy
www.wpda.org
Email: info@wpda.org
Phone: +39 02 66 713 111